Team Sports, Gymnastics, and Dance in Community Settings

A Guide for Teachers, Coaches, and Parents

Patricia A. Sullivan, EdD
Associate Director, HPERD
ERIC Clearinghouse on Teaching
and Teacher Education

HUMAN
KINETICS

Library of Congress Cataloging-in-Publication Data

Team sports, gymnastics, and dance in community settings : a guide for teachers, coaches, and parents / Patricia A. Sullivan, editor (ERIC Clearinghouse on Teacher [sic] and Teacher Education).
   p. cm.
Includes bibliographical references.
ISBN 0-7360-4862-6 (softcover)
   1. Physical education and training—Study and teaching—United States.
   2. Group games—Study and teaching—United States.
   3. Gymnastics—Study and teaching—United States.
   4. Dance—Study and teaching—United States.
   I. Sullivan, Patricia A., 1947- II. ERIC Clearinghouse on Teaching and Teacher Education.
GV365 .T46 2003
796'.07—dc21   2002154304

ISBN: **0-7360-4862-6**

Copyright © 2003 by Human Kinetics Publishers, Inc.

All rights reserved. Except for use in a review, the reproduction or utilization of this work in any form or by any electronic, mechanical, or other means, now known or hereafter invented, including xerography, photocopying, and recording, and in any information storage and retrieval system, is forbidden without the written permission of the publisher.

The Web addresses cited in this text were current as of December 12, 2002.

Acquisitions Editor: Gayle Kassing; **Developmental Editor:** Jennifer L. Walker; **Copyeditor:** Christine M. Drews; **Proofreader:** Red Inc.; **Permission Manager:** Dalene Reeder; **Graphic Designer:** Nancy Rasmus; **Graphic Artists:** Nancy Rasmus and Kathleen Boudreau-Fuoss; **Cover Designer:** Nancy Rasmus; **Photographer (interior):** © Human Kinetics Publishers, Inc. unless otherwise noted; **Printer:** United Graphics

Printed in the United States of America

10 9 8 7 6 5 4 3 2 1

Human Kinetics
Web site: www.HumanKinetics.com

United States: Human Kinetics
P.O. Box 5076
Champaign, IL 61825-5076
800-747-4457
e-mail: humank@hkusa.com

Canada: Human Kinetics
475 Devonshire Road Unit 100
Windsor, ON N8Y 2L5
800-465-7301 (in Canada only)
e-mail: orders@hkcanada.com

Europe: Human Kinetics
107 Bradford Road
Stanningley
Leeds LS28 6AT, United Kingdom
+44 (0) 113 255 5665
e-mail: hk@hkeurope.com

Australia: Human Kinetics
57A Price Avenue
Lower Mitcham, South Australia 5062
08 8277 1555
e-mail: liahka@senet.com.au

New Zealand: Human Kinetics
P.O. Box 105-231, Auckland Central
09-523-3462
e-mail: hkp@ihug.co.nz

The production of this publication has been funded, in part, with Federal funds from the Office of Educational Research and Improvement (OERI), U.S. Department of Education, under contract number ED-99-CO-0007. The content of this publication does not necessarily reflect the views or policies of the U.S. Department of Education nor does mention of trade names, commercial products, or organizations imply endorsement by the U.S. Government.

CONTENTS

Preface — v
Patricia A. Sullivan

Introduction — vii
Liane M. Summerfield

Team Sports — 1
Danny R. Mielke

Gymnastics — 15
Susan M. Tendy
Carmine Giglio

Dance — 35
Gayle Kassing

Appendix: Progression of Physical Activity Skills for Team Sports, Gymnastics, and Dance — 53
About the Contributors — 54
About the Editor — 55

PREFACE

The number and types of instructional physical activity programs available for young people today that are not closely related to our schools is significant. From the perspective of parents, teachers, and coaches it is important for us to select and provide developmentally appropriate programs. Developmentally appropriate instruction takes into account everything we know about how children develop and learn and then matches that information with appropriate content and strategies in the programs we direct. It also assumes that we should treat children as individuals, not as groups, and create the safest possible environments in which to learn. There are many different ways to implement developmentally appropriate programs.

The Educational Resources Information Center (ERIC) Clearinghouse on Teaching and Teacher Education, hosted by the American Association of Colleges of Teacher Education (AACTE) initiated this project to fill a void. Our aim was to help parents, youth sport coaches, and physical activity instructors by providing information on developmentally appropriate instruction in non-school-based dance, gymnastics, and sports programs for students ages 2-18. It is structured according to the following questions:

- What are the most common types of dance, gymnastics, and team sport instruction for children and youth?
- What activities are developmentally appropriate for each age group? What are the benefits and risks for each age group?
- What should parents, instructors, or coaches look for in a dance school, gymnastics program, or team sports program?

It is hoped that this book will enhance understanding of what is important for parents, coaches, and teachers to know when making choices about non-school-based programs for our children. Additional resources and references are provided for those individuals who would like more information on the subject.

Patricia A. Sullivan, EdD
Associate Director, Health, Physical Education, Recreation, and Dance Division
ERIC Clearinghouse on Teaching and Teacher Education

INTRODUCTION

Millions of young people participate in school- or community-based physical activity and sport programs. Because these programs can promote physical fitness, development of motor skills, adoption of an active lifestyle, self-confidence, and social skills, most parents support their children's involvement. In fact, parents are increasingly supporting their children's participation in these activities at younger and younger ages. Children are not small adults, however, and have special needs for safe progression and participation. This publication can guide parents in their search for safe and appropriate activities or sport programs and assist coaches and leaders who want to offer developmentally appropriate activities.

Three types of activities and sport programs are highlighted in this publication as a result of their popularity with children: team sports, gymnastics, and dance. Each chapter provides information useful for selecting an appropriate program, determining if the environment is safe, and assuring that coaches and instructors are qualified. A table provided at the end of this publication indicates an appropriate progression of physical activity skills in team sports, gymnastics, and dance.

Author Danny Mielke presents a chapter on team sports that should interest both parents and coaches. This chapter is applicable to a variety of popular youth sports, including soccer, baseball, softball, basketball, swimming, and martial arts. After discussing what *developmentally appropriate* means, Mielke presents instructional methods for sport programs and describes the content that youth sport programs for children of varying ages should include. With a focus on safety, Mielke suggests criteria for screening coaches and assuring a healthy and safe playing environment.

Susan M. Tendy and Carmine Giglio, accomplished gymnastics instructors, provide valuable information on what progression in gymnastics looks like, from age 18 months to 18 years. Although parents may not have as many choices of gymnastics programs as of team sports, Tendy and Giglio present benchmarks to help parents determine "if this program is right for their children." They thoroughly and concisely discuss age-appropriate activities, benefits of participation, and risk assessment.

Finally, dance specialist Gayle Kassing explores the various settings for dance instruction and what to expect in each type of dance program. Private dance studios, professional and non-professional schools affiliated with dance companies, community recreation and arts departments, and day care and preschool centers are the principal sites for dance instruction. Kassing outlines the types of dance offered in each setting, including movement activities for younger children, and modern, jazz, tap, and ballet for older children. Kassing provides tips to help parents select the right type of dance program and dance teacher.

Parents, instructors, and coaches will find a wealth of information in this concise guide. Putting this knowledge into practice should make youth activity programs safer and more enjoyable for all.

Liane M. Summerfield, PhD
Associate Dean of the School of Health Professions
Chair of the Department of Health and Human Performance
Marymount University, Arlington, Virginia.

TEAM SPORTS

Danny R. Mielke

This chapter discusses the developmentally appropriate practices that should exist in any team sports activity in which children and youth participate. Although the more popular team sports may include soccer, baseball and softball, basketball, ice hockey, and swimming, the recommendations in this chapter relate to any non-school-based team sports activity. Parents can use this information to evaluate and select programs, and sport leaders can use this information to build better programs.

Overview of Developmentally Appropriate Concepts

Children are often characterized as being intrinsically motivated and self-directed. To effectively teach sports skills to children, instructors must capitalize on this intrinsic motivation. Activities will work best when children are allowed to explore, experiment, and critically analyze the many and varied movement experiences they receive.

Developmentally appropriate practices traditionally reflect an interactive and often constructivist view of learning. Developmental theorists such as Dewey, Vygotsky, Piaget, and Erikson are often associated with this perspective. The key principle in this approach is that children build their own knowledge through interactions with their social and physical environments. Children are active participants in their own development (Bredekamp 1992; Novak 1996).

The role of the coach or leader can be described more as a facilitator who "creates a natural moment" (Vygotsky 1978) in children's environments. The coach becomes a "dispenser of occasions" (Phillips 1993) rather than someone who merely distributes information. Within a developmentally appropriate context, learning must include practices that reflect both the age-appropriate and individual needs of children.

The following chart gives an example of the differences a parent might see in an age-appropriate youth sport setting. In general, children ages 4 to 8 would learn the fundamental skills of the particular sport through basic skills instruction, while applying those skills in mini-games and fun activities. Highly competitive activity would not be emphasized. Children ages 9 to 12 would begin to apply ba-

Developmental Expectations for Ball Control Skills in a Youth Sport Setting

Ages 4-8	Ages 9-12
Throwing skills	
Throw a ball using a contralateral pattern with trunk rotation and follow-through with a partner or small group.	Using a contralateral pattern with trunk rotation and follow-through, throw overhand with force using distance and accuracy in an applied setting.
Kicking skills	
Kick a stationary ball using the instep of the foot as the contact surface.	Kick a moving ball and punt a ball with force and accuracy in an applied game setting.
Catching skills	
Catch a gently thrown ball with the hands while demonstrating ability to absorb force with flexible knees, elbows and other body parts.	Catch a ball with the hands while moving in an applied game setting.
Striking skills	
Strike a stationary ball or self-tossed ball using various body parts, a bat, a paddle, or a racquet.	Strike a moving ball with a body part (as in volleyball), a bat, a paddle, or a racquet demonstrating force and accuracy.

sic skills and learn more advanced ones; they would use these skills in competitive situations.

Skill and Fitness Development for Participation in Sport

"Motor fitness can be described as the process of performing quality fundamental motor skills at a developmentally appropriate level. From a practical perspective, the acquisition of fundamental motor skills (functional movement ability) is a prerequisite to participation in physical activity" (Mielke 1993). The first priority of any youth sport program is teaching the fundamental movement skills of the activity. Achieving skill awareness and competence will promote a child's interest in developing and maintaining the physical skills and fitness necessary to participate in sport activity.

It is essential to develop physical fitness before participating in a sport and to maintain fitness as an integral part of a continuing sport program. The National Association for Sport and Physical Education (NASPE 1992) provides the following guidelines to determine if a sport participant might be "physically educated":

- The participant has the skills necessary to perform a wide variety of physical and sport activities.
- The participant is physically fit as indicated by his or her performance on tests that measure fitness components.
- The participant chooses to be involved in regular vigorous physical activity, being physically active at least three times a week.
- The participant is aware of the implications and benefits associated with regular physical activity.
- The participant values physical activity and its contribution to a healthy lifestyle.

These five outcomes are not typically associated with youth sport, and yet these principles are of paramount importance if children and young people are going to derive significant benefits from their participation in sport. The extent of the sport leader's preparation of the young athlete in skill and fitness will have a significant impact on the child's enjoyment and success in the activity.

Promoting Self-Worth

Self-esteem, often called self-worth, is defined as how we judge our worthiness and indicates the extent to which individuals believe themselves to be capable, significant, successful, and worthy (Coopersmith 1967). To promote self-worth in the youth sport environment, leaders must modify the sport activity appropriately. Eliminating excessive physical contact in youth ice hockey, reducing the size of the playing area, and reducing the duration of contests are examples of modifying sports to better match the characteristics of children and youth. Other modifications include reducing the height of the basket to improve the possibility for success in basketball, granting a point if a child's shot hits the rim in basketball, or enlarging the goal in soccer.

In addition to promoting self-esteem by altering many of the physical components of sport, self-worth can be encouraged by allowing all children to participate equally in the activity. If a child is selected to be a member of a team, then the child should have an opportunity to play in all scheduled contests. Of course, the child should also be expected to attend practices, participate cooperatively, and work to learn new skills.

The development of appropriate social behavior begins at birth, well before a child's initiation into sport. Parents, siblings, family, and friends provide important information to infants, toddlers, and young children about acceptable ways to act in a sport setting. Children learn that physical actions such as biting, hitting, pinching, and kicking are not acceptable choices because these actions can hurt others (Ewing 1997). Through sport, children can learn that there are rules and limits regarding behavior. They learn that being treated with dignity requires treating others likewise.

Teaching Sport Concepts

Traditional sport classes, as taught in school physical education programs, typically use skill drills to teach individual components of the sport and then hold team tournaments to practice the skills in a game environment. In such a setting, sport is decontextualized, and students are not truly educated in sport. When sport is taught well, children are provided developmentally appropriate experiences through increased playing competence, personal and social growth, and taking responsibility for their own sport experience (Tannehill 2000).

In an ideal community-based sport activity, team affiliation and cohesion are emphasized along with sports skills. Participants engage in a season of some moderate length during which there is time to improve personal skills. Formal competition between teams occurs, records are kept, and a culminating event, frequently a championship, is held, which provides feedback and recognition. The sport season provides a festive atmosphere that enhances personal enjoyment and allows for the celebration of traditions unique to the sport. All the events are conducted in a way that provides support for the developmental level of the participants.

The size of a youth sport program will vary based on the sport activity and the number of players who can be on the court or field. Although no set guidelines exist, the ratio of players to coaches should not exceed 17 to 1. Having at least two coaches is optimal in most settings and should be required if the number of players exceeds 17.

In developmentally appropriate sport and activity settings, children typically learn motor skills in a sequential, age-appropriate manner (Grineski 1992). Presenting skills that are either too advanced or too simple can be frustrating for all involved.

Different Approaches to Teaching Children

Experts have recommended that within school settings, children should be allowed free exploration and personal responses to a wide array of tasks (Barrett, Williams, and Whitall 1992). Children should be allowed to work at their own individual level, which lets them experience success through displays of competence in their movement. Adhering to the same suggestions in a sport setting will facilitate an equally successful experience.

Skills should be presented through both direct and indirect forms of teaching. Coaches commonly teach skills by having children repeat a prescribed example. However, when appropriate, an indirect style such as guided discovery can allow participants to explore movement options and arrive at the most effective way to perform the skill.

In addition, skills presentation in team sports should exhibit progression. For example, in a ball throwing activity, children will not be able to effectively throw to a moving partner unless they have first learned the more basic skill of throwing a ball to a stationary partner.

Modifications to traditional games, such as basketball or soccer, may be necessary to accommodate individual differences. An instructor may reduce the team size to three players or not use a goalkeeper. In this way all children can be more actively involved.

The instructor must give equal opportunity to every child on the team, regardless of skill level. Providing considerable time for learning motor skills, allowing adequate skills practice time, and consolidating skills at each child's level are important goals of a developmentally appropriate sport curriculum.

Program Content

Youth sport directors, parents, and community leaders should consider several important concepts when developing or selecting a well-balanced and effective program. Effective non-school-based youth sport programs are generally marked by appropriate levels of competition, clear performance expectations, the matching of maturity among participants, careful screening of adult leaders, formative assessments of the participants, and a healthy and safe environment.

Participation and Performance Expectations

All children, regardless of skill level or disability, should be allowed to actively participate in sport activities. In a developmentally appropriate situation, children and young people are active throughout the lesson, practice, or competition. Competitive levels are aligned on the basis of each child's proficiency in the skill demands of the sport. At very young ages (under 10), sport should be open and accessible to all interested children. As children age and opportunities arise for some children to become involved in more specialized team activities such as select or traveling programs, other opportunities should still be afforded to those youth who wish to participate in a less competitive or less selective environment.

Sport activities need to have a coherent course of study with goals and objectives that will be achieved through participation in the particular activity. Expectations should be appropriate for the age level but need to be challenging and reflect the high level of interest that the students have in sport and recreational activities. For example, a youth sport basketball program should identify what level of skill each child is expected to gain during the season for dribbling and shooting. There should be a tangible measure of the success of that claim. And the product should reflect the developmental level of the child.

Instructors should establish performance expectations that focus on allowing children to participate at their own levels. This means that the practice or training session should be a learning experience. Children will make errors, and the coaches will make corrections by reteaching the skills. The adults should never cause the children to feel demeaned or abused. The children are in a developmental stage in which they should be permitted to make novice mistakes that are not ridiculed.

As a general rule, preschool children should not engage in competitive sport activities but should be learning fundamental individual skills with brief experiences in whole-group activity. When young children become involved in competitive sport at too early an age, they typically do not have the requisite skills and become either passive observers or discouraged participants, neither of which meets the objectives of the sport program.

Participants' Maturity and Ability

In most cases, youth sport is organized by chronological age. Two children whose ages are 10.0 and 10.9 years are typically classified as 10 years of age, although almost one year separates the two. This age difference may have a significant effect on the ability of these children to participate on an equal basis. Cutoff dates for participation in a sport should reflect such chronological differences (Malina 2000).

Variations in size, biological maturity, strength, skill, and behavior (i.e., social, emotional, and cognitive development) during many phases of children's development can be considerable. Matching participants by body size and biological maturity is often indicated as a means of equalizing competition to reduce the risk of injury and increase the possibility of success (Malina 2000). Skill levels may also be considered in some cases.

Recently, some have advocated the use of self-assessment of sexual maturation for maturity matching in youth sport. This format is increasingly used in clinical studies and could work well in team sports. Sexual maturation and the growth spurt are highly variable among girls and boys in terms of when they occur and how rapidly or slowly youth progress through the processes (Malina 2000). The ages when girls and boys develop secondary sex characteristics can be used to determine an appropriate maturational alignment for sport participants. At a recent youth soccer game, the author witnessed a contest where one team's players ranged in age from 9 to 13 while the other group was mostly 10-year-olds. Despite the differences in age and size, the skills of the participants were similar and made for an exciting and competitive situation.

Adult Leadership

The sponsorship of youth sport in the United States depends largely on community service organizations that rely primarily on volunteers to conduct their programs. Sponsors of youth sport programs have a special obligation to protect the health and well-being of their young participants.

Volunteer coaches are difficult to recruit and retain because of the significant time commitment required for practices and contests. Most people who become involved in coaching have little or no formal training in child development. Although willing, these coaches have had few, if any, experiences with children and youth in the context of sport and in the assessment of skill. These volunteer coaches and program leaders are often parents who have little training in the fundamental concepts of the sport or in child development.

Seefeldt (1999) suggested some screening tools to assist in the selection of qualified adult coaches. These levels of review can be used to evaluate the suitability of volunteers and staff in youth sport programs. Potential coaches should adequately meet the requirements of all levels of screening.

The first level of screening is an application form that includes complete identification, qualifications, experience, background, references, waiver and consent to conduct specific background checks, and the applicant's signature. Of the position requirements, perhaps the applicant's experience in developmentally appropriate practices should be weighted most heavily. Individuals can gain this type of developmentally appropriate instructional skill through formal higher education or through various coaching training programs such as the Program for Athletes and Coaches Education (PACE) or the American Sport Education Program (ASEP).

The second level of screening involves a personal interview. Program administrators should have a written job description describing the demands of the position and the vulnerability of the clients to be served. The job description can be presented in the interview and serve as the basis for questions. Interviewers should pay special attention to the applicant's understanding of how to work with children in developmentally appropriate ways.

The third level of screening involves investigating areas of a personal nature, including abuse of drugs and alcohol, sexual offenses, violations of the law involving motor vehicles, physical examinations, and a test for HIV. Administrators should inform and receive consent from applicants for such tests before initiating the third level of screening.

The final level of screening is the performance assessment of volunteers and employees, which should be an ongoing part of supervision. Such scrutiny is most likely to occur when the actions of a volunteer or employee have aroused the ire, suspicion, or distrust of parents or participants. However, performance evaluation should instead be an ongoing process, to provide both positive and constructive feedback to personnel. Performance evaluations must be conducted without bias regarding gender, race, creed, religious affiliation, or other classification. Administrators or program directors should use the written job description as the basis for judgment, comparing volunteers' or employees' performance to the expectations outlined in the job description. Written documentation of areas in which the performance fails to meet the mandatory standard of care prescribed by the organization should be available to the personnel under scrutiny. In keeping with the intent of developmentally appropriate programs, perhaps the focus of ongoing evaluation could be, "Did this volunteer display developmentally appropriate skills in his or her work with children?"

Assessment

Adults working with children's programs should regularly assess the progress of the students involved in their programs. Typically, assessments are conducted on an informal basis where the participants' performances are observed during practice or competitive situations. Instead assessments should be based on formative, ongoing evaluations of each child or young adult and should not be used only to determine who starts a game or who gets cut from a team.

The results of evaluations should form the basis for the type of instruction that students receive during coaching sessions. The adult and child should review the performance evaluation together and set goals for improvement. With the coach's assistance, children can meet their goals for participation.

Creating a Healthy and Safe Environment

The playing environment should be carefully screened. Instructors should visually survey the facility and note any concerns. Obvious hazards might include bleachers, wall protrusions, or poor floor quality. In many cases it might be necessary to take specific precautions such as padding walls or doors, removing dangerous hazards, or replacing and repairing equipment or facilities.

Instructors might also interview the facility manager and check on maintenance schedules and upkeep plans. Parents should discuss with the director any concerns regarding the safety of the facilities.

One aspect of a safe environment includes using developmentally appropriate sizes and types of equipment. Using smaller or larger balls, colorful balls, or balls marked with numbers or letters may help facilitate learning for children and young people.

Using equipment and facilities that are not developmentally appropriate could lead to injury and reduced success for the participants. Simply putting children into an adult-sized environment is not best for the development of the child. Instead, instructors and leaders should try to create a unique space for the developmental level of the children and the sport or recreational activity for which they are preparing.

Risk Assessment

When parents send a child to participate in a youth sport activity they should understand that the child is participating in a voluntary activity where there is a chance of injury. Coaches should also clarify risks involved in specific sports. Wise parents and participants should understand the risk they are assuming and take precautions to protect themselves. Throughout this chapter, the leadership necessary for successful youth sport, the importance of proper equipment and facilities, and the importance of developmentally appropriate practices have been discussed. Youth sport participants need to examine all parameters of the sport environment they choose and make sure risk is minimized.

Sport Camps

Sport camps vary greatly, and parents should consider several components before selecting a sport camp for their child. Considerations include cost, location, and coach qualifications and the child's age, skill, and ambition.

Sport camps generally are offered as either day camps or residential camps. In day camps, the children will attend only during the day and will return home at night; in residential camps, the children will remain overnight. Initially, choosing a day or residential camp may depend on proximity to the camp. Residential fees, because they include room and board, will exceed day camp cost. However, of primary concern should be the kind of supervision children receive outside the actual sport camp activities. It can be a meaningful childhood experience to attend a residential sport camp if the whole experience, both day and night, is structured and safe.

Before choosing a camp, parents should ask several questions regarding the camp leadership. Who is coaching the camp? Does the head coach have specific academic qualifications or sport certifications that establish his or her expertise? Who will be assisting the head coach? Many sport camps are sponsored by schools and universities. Often the assistant coaches are students from that school who, although they usually have a lot of enthusiasm, may not be trained or prepared to coach the activity. Other parents may be able to offer recommendations of appropriate sport camps in the area.

Finally, parents should consider the age, skill, and ambition of the child. For young children, attendance at a camp should revolve around the child's desire to improve his or her sport-specific skills, be with friends, and have fun. The child should want to be there! Children under age 10 should probably attend half-day or full-day camps rather than residential camps.

A residential camp or a multiple-day camp in the community might be appropriate for older children who are serious about dedicating time to a specific sport. These camps are more appropriate for middle school, junior high, and high school athletes rather than for younger children.

Summary

Successful developmentally appropriate sport programs for children require several key components. Effective teaching, appropriate skill content, qualified leaders, proper assessment, and promotion of fitness and self-worth are all necessary to ensure a good experience for children in sport. Parents should seek out appropriate experiences and sport leaders. Coaches and other adults working with children in team sports should adhere to appropriate developmental guidelines.

References

Barrett, K.R., K. Williams, and J. Whitall. 1992. What does it mean to have a "developmentally appropriate physical education program"? *Physical Educator* 49 (3): 114-118.

Bredekamp, S. 1992. What is developmentally appropriate and why is it important? *Journal of Physical Education, Recreation and Dance* 63 (6): 31-32.

Coopersmith, S. 1967. The antecedents of self-esteem. San Francisco: W.H. Freeman.

Ewing, M. 1997. Promoting social and moral development through sports. [Online]. Available: http://ed-web3.educ.msu.edu/ysi/Spotlights.htm.

Grineski, S. 1992. What is a truly developmentally appropriate physical education program for children? *Journal of Physical Education, Recreation and Dance* 63 (6): 33-35.

Malina, R. 2000. Matching youth in sport by maturity status. [Online]. Available: http://ed-web3.educ.msu.edu/ysi/Spotlights.htm.

Mielke, D. 1993. Motor fitness: A precursor to physical fitness. In *Healthy from the start: New perspectives on childhood fitness*. Washington, DC: ERIC Clearinghouse on Teaching and Teacher Education.

National Association for Sport and Physical Education. 1992. *Outcomes of quality physical education programs.* Reston, VA: American Alliance for Health, Physical Education, Recreation and Dance.

Novak, R. 1996. Developmentally appropriate and culturally responsive education: Theory in practice. Northwest Regional Educational Lab. [Online]. Available: http://www.nwrel.org/cfc/publications/dap2.html.

Phillips, C.B. 1993. The hundred languages of children. *Young Children* 49 (1): 17-18.

Seefeldt, V. 1999. Selecting and screening volunteer coaches for youth programs. [Online]. Available: http://ed-web3.educ.msu.edu/ysi/Spotlights.htm.

Tannehill, D. 2000. Sport education workshop. [Online]. Available: http://www.pelinks4u.org/profdevel/sportedwk.htm.

Vygotsky, L.S. 1978. *Mind in society.* Cambridge, MA: Harvard University Press.

GYMNASTICS

Susan M. Tendy
Carmine Giglio

Gymnastics and related movement activities offer great opportunities for children to develop skill-related components of fitness: flexibility, balance, coordination, upper-body and abdominal strength, and kinesthetic awareness. These basic skills will give children a head start in their movement careers no matter what activity they eventually choose to pursue. In addition to selecting the level of involvement for their children, whether recreational or competitive, parents must consider many other aspects of the sport of gymnastics. This section provides a gymnastics primer for parents, including a guide to resources for further information.

Selecting a Program for Your Child

Most communities have a variety of opportunities for team sports involvement. In contrast, some communities have only one gymnastics program. Additionally, the number of school systems offering gymnastics instruction is declining. Therefore, non-school-based programs are carrying the banner for the survival of the sport. Because non-school-based gymnastics programs are not regulated, parents must ask questions and become involved in the development of their child's program. Most gymnastics schools have a booster club composed of parents and interested supporters who handle many of the organizational aspects for the coach. This organization, or the manager for each club, should be able to supply basic information to all potential clients. Inquiring clients, as potential future members of the booster club, can make an impact on the development and direction of the organization. Parental involvement and support is an important key to the success of every club.

Nevertheless, how does a parent decide where to go, what to do, and whom to trust? When selecting a gymnastics program for a child, parents should consider essential factors such as teaching and coaching staff experience, attendance and safety policies, insurance coverage, and facility maintenance. These behind-the-scenes indicators will reveal whether the organization is grounded in the professional attention to detail that is necessary for successful program operation. Parents should visit the facility at which the club practices. The following list of considerations can help to evaluate the organization:

- Instructors should have earned a coaching accreditation and safety certification through a recognized national organization, such as USA Gymnastics. These certificates should be on display, or available on file, and up-to-date.
- Safety awareness should be evident, as indicated by signs, safety mats, posted emergency procedures, and accessible telephones.
- Spotting awareness should be evident: A child should never practice an event unsupervised. Observers may see older, more experienced teammates acting as spotters for simple skills, but a well-positioned, vigilant coach (or two) is a must for the more difficult moves.
- Proper lead-up techniques should be introduced: New events are not taught or attempted until the basic foundational skills have been introduced and mastered.
- Equipment should be fairly new and properly maintained.
- The workout and changing room areas should be clean.
- The overall facility should be well lit, both inside and out. Good outdoor lighting is especially important for parents and athletes attending early and late classes.
- Club insurance policies should be open for inspection, provide coverage for all ages of participants, and include coverage for the use of all training equipment in the building, including trampolines.
- At the competitive level, parents may compare the team's performance against other teams in the area or region. This might be a reflection of the quality of instruction.

Parents should also evaluate the range of recreational and competitive levels within the organization. Many gymnastics schools focus on the younger age groups but not the older, more experienced gymnast. There is nothing wrong with this approach; in fact, it allows the school to better focus the talents of its staff. However, ideally a child should be able to stay with one club, and progress through and choose from the different developmental levels offered by the program, throughout his or her career.

Observing the practice sessions of more experienced athletes affords wonderful role modeling and motivational opportunities for young gymnasts. A program that exposes young gymnasts to advanced skill levels may also allow the child already comfortable with the facility, coaching staff, and cohort group to successfully meet the new challenge of skill advancement. The following section gives an overview of the various stages of participation and progress, based on ability and age.

Developmental Divisions and Age-Group Categories

A common introduction to the gymnastics world is a developmental class for very young children, to which parents are often invited. However, children have not been left at the starting gate if they have not experienced the "mommy and me" gymnastics classes for 3-year-olds and under. Most gymnastics schools have entry-level classes for older youth. In fact, the better programs accommodate varying developmental stages of all participants. Many schools include age groups within the various ability levels.

Most clubs organize their activities around three participation categories. These categories and their levels are as follows:

Preschool gymnastics
  Parent and tot (18-month-olds to 3-year-olds)
  Preschool (4- and 5-year-olds)

Team gymnastics (6- to 18-year-olds)
  Preteam
  Team

Recreational gymnastics (6- to 18-year-olds)
  Beginner
  Intermediate
  Advanced

Members of recreational classes who demonstrate exceptional talent can further their experience through participating in team level activities. Additionally, various national and international organizations have a published system of ability levels and corresponding age categories for routines at these levels.

Age-Appropriate Activities

Many basic activities form the foundation for the future development of a well-rounded athlete. Parents should allow their children to explore their changing levels of interest as they develop. Participating in a program that includes a wide variety of supplemental activities will not only enhance the overall ability of the youngster, but also allow for the child's natural curiosity to be addressed. The appendix at the back of this publication provides a table that summarizes the types of activities that may be introduced at various age levels. Remember, not all athletes develop at the same time or at the same rate. Many qualities—including age, body type, determination, strength, and attention span—affect a child's progression. Club coaches, through their coaching education certification courses, have been trained to account for these differences in ability. Additionally, mastery of introductory or lead-up skills is essential for safe and successful progression. Keeping this in mind, the following discussion explains when activities should be introduced.

Kinesthetic Awareness Exercises: Rolling, Twisting, and Turning

18-month-olds to 3-year-olds

Discussion

At this age, parents attend the class with their children. Parents are often seated in a circle, with their children in front of them, facing center. Children are never too young to be taught the importance of a warm-up, and dedicating time at the beginning of each session is an important activity to develop good habits. At this age, basic, repetitive, nonimpact major body movements can accomplish the goals of a warm-up.

Parent and tot programs should include games and activities that allow for creative movement exploration and body awareness. Rolling, twisting, and turning activities in a play atmosphere will allow the child to discover where he or she is in relation to the space around him or her. These movement activities require more balance and control than one might typically expect from a young child (Gallahue and

Ozmun 1998, 217-218). Therefore, parental understanding of the various stages of development, and patience during these stages, is important. For example, initial rolling attempts may lack the stability, balance, and transition skills needed when changing levels. As the child's technique matures, the ability to maintain control and transition into another movement will become evident. Small hoops and balls allow young students to experience skills involving eye–hand coordination.

Benefits
Development of spatial awareness.

Risk Assessment
Ensure that matting is present and does not interfere with movement activities.

Basic Gymnastics Skills: Body Position, Tightness, and Control
18-month-olds to 3-year-olds

Discussion
Infants begin to stretch, reach, and make contact with objects at about 5 months of age. At about 10 months, most children can pull themselves up to a standing position (Gallahue and Ozmun 1998, 210). This is evidence that in addition to curiosity, a basic strength component is developing. Therefore, by the time a child is ready for the toddler classes, parent and child will be able to participate together in simple imitative movements that involve static stretching and balance activities. Pulling or climbing up to a standing position from a seated position, holding a stretch, stretching the arms overhead, holding the legs together and straight, and so forth, can be accomplished with a walking or crawling toddler. The parent may support the child for balance, hold the child for total support, or allow a child to stand unsupported if able.

Benefits
Development of body position, alignment, and control.

Risk Assessment
Ensure that the child's weight is supported and that he or she is carefully spotted during any pulling or hanging movements. This will prevent falling and shoulder dislocations caused by a relatively low strength-to-weight ratio.

Flexibility Training
18-month-olds to 3-year-olds

Discussion
Children are naturally flexible. Many parent and tot programs include basic stretching movements, and these are probably as beneficial for the parent as for the child. Instructors may use imagery and games to help the child mimic the movements to be learned. For example, to encourage stretching forward in the seated straddle position, the cue "pretend you are making a sandwich, and smoothing jelly on the bread" might help the child to understand the importance of using the arms to stretch forward. Activity stations can also be set up, and the transition time between stations may be seen as a break for the child.

Benefits
Working with the natural elasticity of the child to develop awareness of stretching and strengthening movements, while being aware of the low level of muscular strength at this point in a child's development, is a good first step to developing the flexibility needed for both injury prevention and performance.

Risk Assessment
The natural flexibility of a child should not be exploited, as injury can result from causing a joint to move beyond its natural range of motion.

General Fitness Skills: Running and Jumping
4- and 5-year-olds

Discussion

Somewhere between the ages of 2 and 3, a child will develop the ability to run, wherein a phase of air time (both feet off the ground at the same point) can actually be observed. At about 3 years of age, a child will likely develop a recognizable stride. At about 4 years of age, a child will begin to show some control of running and jumping. And at about 5 years of age, a child will begin to demonstrate and control a true running gait. At about this point in time, a child will begin to develop the power needed to initiate a jump or spring, along with the basic muscle strength needed to slow down the descent (Gallahue and Ozmun 1998, 212).

Many techniques can safely help young children learn the control skills needed to jump and land safely. Trampoline techniques are gentle on the developing leg bones and knee joints. Basic trampoline activities can help the young child learn proper jumping and landing techniques and develop the beginning levels of leg power and control needed in gymnastics.

The young child can also begin to develop a correct and efficient running form. Practicing the elements of basic stride and arm pumping form during short relay races of various types can aid in the development and improvement of running efficiency and technique.

Benefits

Trampoline activities help develop plyometric ability, which can be described as the power and technique involved in jumping and landing safely. The muscles stretch as they are loaded by the downward force of the body, for example, flexing at the hips, knees, and ankles while preparing for a jump. The muscles then immediately contract to leap up off the floor or the trampoline. Upon landing, the leg muscles contract to control the downward force of the body.

Risk Assessment

Young bones are still developing. Uncontrolled landing from even a moderate height should be discouraged. As the running gait gradually develops, so too the plyometric strength to power up and soften the landing gradually develops. Gradual development is key, and research indicates that parents and instructors should err on the side of caution when teaching running and jumping (Caine and Lindner 1985).

Tumbling

6- and 7-year-olds

Discussion

Basic tumbling activities can start at a young age, with allowances for a young child's lack of the plyometric ability needed to jump and land onto either the hands or the feet under control. Preschool and young students might begin with very basic rolling activities, for example, simple side rolls. Gradually, forward and backward rolls, cartwheels, lunge handstands with a spotter, and full handstands against a wall will be taught to the 6- and 7-year-old groups. Round-offs and front handsprings will be taught as students progress. A child may not learn these skills until he or she has moved up to the next age group or developed the strength and power needed for such activities. Many young children rapidly increase in skill level, yet many older athletes begin their gymnastics careers as late as ages 7 to 10 and do just fine.

Jumping skills such as tuck and straddle jumps and half- and full-turn jumps help children develop the power needed for vaulting. As skill ability progresses, these jumping skills will serve as the basis for somersault variations. Tumbling skills are taught and practiced well into a gymnast's career. "Add-a-Trick" is a fun game that provides tumbling transition experience and can be played at almost any level. The child is given an initial task by observing a visual model of one movement, volunteered by a teammate of similar ability. The child then performs that skill, and adds one more of his or her choice. The initial partner then adds a third "trick" to the two already sequenced. This can continue back and forth until a preset number of skills is reached, one partner forgets the sequence, or time is called. Only skills already mastered by both partners should be used.

Benefits

Tumbling skills are the bread and butter of a gymnast's repertoire. They can be taught to large groups with maximum activity and minimal equipment; activity level is high, and waiting time is less. Kinesthetic awareness and control while inverted or airborne is an essential quality that will improve with increased tumbling experience.

Risk Assessment

Headstands must not be done at a younger age, as vertebrae and supportive neck muscles are still developing. Spotting is very important for activities requiring the body to be completely supported by the arms until the student is strong enough to control these skills. Handsprings in particular should be carefully spotted by the coach. Back handsprings and somersaults are taught to the older students (8- to 12-year-old groups) as their strength develops, but beginning lead-ups are often introduced at the 6- to 7-year-old level.

Trampoline Activities

6- and 7-year-olds

Discussion

Basic jumping activities come naturally, as parents whose children jump on their bed can attest to. When safely taught and carefully monitored, trampoline activities can greatly benefit the development of body position, kinesthetic awareness, and control in the vertical world. After learning how to safely get on and off of a trampoline, children will learn basic bouncing and the "check" bounce (controlled stop). Young children can also learn basic seat drops and the proper landing position for these. Six- and 7-year-olds can learn a jump half-turn to a check bounce. As leg power develops in the 8 and older group, a seat drop half-turn to a seat drop, also known as a "swivel hips," can be taught. Front drops and back drops might be taught to the 8- to 12-year-old groups.

For the 13- to 18-year-old groups, somersaulting in either a forward or backward direction requires a spotting belt. These tricks should be spotted only by the coach. A spotting belt allows for simultaneous twisting and somersaulting movements and can also be used for floor work. Divers and figure skaters also use trampoline and twisting belt training, and skaters use spotting belts on the ice.

Benefits

Compared with floor work, trampoline work allows for less impact on the legs and more airtime, simulating the acrobatic situations needed in the gymnast's repertoire.

Risk Assessment

Trampoline activities are the easiest gymnastics skills to master, yet they can lead to high rates of injury if not monitored properly. Students must be taught respect for this simple piece of equipment. An instructor must be present during all trampoline activities. Spotters must be stationed at every open end of the trampoline. No horseplay should be allowed. Basic safety instruction in getting on and off the trampoline will prevent inadvertent injuries. To mount the trampoline, students should climb onto the frame. While on the trampoline, all jumping and stopping should be controlled. To dismount, students should stop jumping, crouch down, sit on the frame with the feet forward, and slither off like a snake. Following these basic rules and showing respect for the trampoline will ensure a safe learning experience.

Ballet and Dance Lessons

6- and 7-year-olds

Discussion

Dance training will help a young gymnast develop awareness of correct body alignment, control, balance, and style. Experts feel that these skills will result in fewer injuries. Ballet lessons add to the style and grace of the gymnast, especially in the tumbling and balance beam events.

According to Biggs and Judge (1998), common dance skills that can be directly applied to gymnastics include the following:

Body alignment—Flat back, tight abdomen

Battement —Foot push-offs to fast leg drives through a full range of motion

Battement tendu—Leg extension with the toe pointed and in contact with the floor

Demi-plié—Slight knee bend with heels in contact with the ground for Achilles flexibility and upper-leg development and control

Benefits

The ability to control a landing and the limb speed and explosive power gained from ballet training over time will certainly enhance a gymnast's tumbling skills. Ballet training at an early age provides merely an introduction to the basics, including body alignment and flexibility.

Risk Assessment

Dance classes designed for young children should be fun. Group lessons offer the social benefit of allowing children to meet others with similar interests. Parents should be patient with their child's developmental progress, however, and remember that each child develops differently. Comparing one child to another may put a child in a position to try things too early for his or her particular level.

Agility Drills

6- and 7-year-olds

Discussion

Games, stunts, and relays can be used as avenues for agility training. Instructors can use animal names as imagery for individual stunts with the younger groups. As students mature, a competitive atmosphere can be introduced by recording personal bests or organizing relay races that require the completion of agility tasks.

The following activities are some examples of noncompetitive stunts that can be developed into relays as the students progress (Fait 1964).

Frog hop: Squat with hands on the floor; jump and land like a frog.

Crab walk: Place hands and feet on the floor, body facing up. Walk forward and backward using hands and feet in opposition.

Gymnastics

Bear walk: Place hands and feet on the floor, body facing down. Walk forward and backward moving the hands and feet on the same side of the body simultaneously.

Seal walk: Assume a push-up position with the toes pointed. Walk forward on the hands while dragging the legs.

Inchworm: Place hands and feet on the floor, body facing down. Alternate walking the hands away from the feet into a fully extended body position, then walking the feet in toward the hands to a pike position.

Low crawl: Slide on the abdomen, using the hands and feet to propel oneself forward.

The following activities can be set up as relay races or as individually timed or scored events, whereby the child competes as a member of a small team or against a prior personal performance:

From here to there: Repeat a series of skills (e.g., dive rolls or cartwheel passes) across the floor exercise mat.

Over and under obstacle course: Depending on ability level, alternate climbing or vaulting over an obstacle with crawling or rolling under an obstacle. Safety hint: Use rolled-up mats, apparatus, and existing equipment with which athletes are familiar.

Circle or tire drill: Mark off two rows of circles about the size of a car tire, staggering the placement so that each circle is offset halfway from the tires adjacent to it. Have athletes initially step only one foot within each circle without touching the lines. Progress to a pump-and-lift movement with the arms and legs so that the body is lifted off the ground. Advanced gymnasts can attempt to walk on their hands from one circle to the next, one hand within each circle.

Benefits

Agility-type drills that utilize total body movements in a gamelike setting will help to keep the fun in practices, while developing an essential gross motor coordination base. Once a basic movement is learned, evaluating the performance in a nonthreatening manner will help to maintain motivation and self-esteem. Learning and performing more complex skills involves absorbing and reacting to information such as movement demands (speed, direction, and force) and available feedback (Martens 1997). These games and activities supply the feedback needed to help the learner improve.

Risk Assessment

When introducing skills, coaches need to set up the teaching situation so that optimal learning will take place. Each skill should be

introduced safely—instructors should have students' attention;

demonstrated correctly—instructors may use a more experienced athlete or a video;

practiced safely—complex combinations should be broken down and lead-ups should be used;

assessed to provide feedback—feedback can occur through coaching observation, skill analysis, and athlete self-reflection during performance and through using gamelike techniques (Martens 1997).

General Strength Skills: Pull-ups, Sit-ups, and Push-ups

8- and 12-year-olds

Discussion

Opportunities for climbing can be encouraged on small, low ladders and bars. Modified dips, push-ups, and pull-ups can be introduced for upper-body development. Abdominal strength work can begin with crunches.

Benefits

Strength training for gymnastics by doing basic movements utilizing one's own body weight is beneficial for developing children. Activity modifications based on ability will enable all athletes to experience success within their group while educating them as to the next possible level of performance.

Risk Assessment

Strength training for young children should not include free weights. Additionally, activities such as dips should be carefully supervised or modified, to avoid elbow tendinitis and shoulder stress. The dip activity can be modified by having the child sit in a reverse dip or "L" position with the heels on the floor and the hands on a 6- to 12-inch raised step or platform behind the child. The lever length of the legs can be shortened by placing an additional fulcrum or balance point such as a small rolled-up foam padding tube under the knees or thighs (instead of using the heels on the floor as the fulcrum).

Skill-Specific Body, Trunk, and Leg Circuit Training

8- to 12-year-olds

Discussion

Circuit stations can facilitate training and maintain motivation. Strength training with anything other than body weight should be done only by the older age groups (17- and 18-year-olds). However, as an opportunity for practicing various skills at all age levels, stations can be set up in a gym, with pre-recorded musical time segments signifying the amount of time groups can work at a station. When the music stops, the gymnasts rotate to the next station, and the tape includes a corresponding quiet time to allow time to switch stations. This lets the coach focus on teaching and skills management rather than keeping track of a stopwatch. It also forces athletes to move to the next station within a certain time limit. If advanced skills, such as preparation for an Iron Cross, are being worked on, a station can be set up so that the gymnast goes through the movement with no resistance at all, and then with assistance or with a spotter. Younger age groups can use the circuit philosophy to practice lead-ups for a skill that they are working on or to practice skills already learned. For example, the handstand could have four separate stations reflecting various ability levels or assistance needed: three-quarter modified balance, handstand against a wall, handstand with a spotter, and free handstand.

Benefits

Circuit stations increase time on task and help gymnasts focus on a particular task for a specific amount of time. Playing popular music as a background signal provides a good motivational tool for all ages. The athletes may even make suggestions as to what type of music they want to hear!

Risk Assessment

Every station must be constantly monitored. This monitoring can be facilitated through a preliminary organizational briefing to the group. The leader can explain and demonstrate the correct technique expected at each station to the entire group before athletes start the circuit. This will free up the instructor or coach to monitor several stations at once, knowing that the entire group has been taught the requirements of each station.

Signs and diagrams should be posted at each station to remind athletes what they are supposed to do. This will prevent the gymnasts from practicing something that has not been taught. Signs could also be used to indicate that the first time through the station a certain lead-up skill is practiced, and the second time through the circuit a higher-level related skill is performed. To allow recovery time, stations should be organized so that upper-body strength skills are alternated with lower-body or tumbling activities.

Summary

"Olympians were not made in a day; otherwise we would all be on the team."
—Susan M. Tendy

I often make the remark above to motivate young athletes who become impatient to master a difficult skill. I also challenge parents to remember that achieving true excellence requires perserverance and development over time. Parents may discover new dimensions of responsibility and be tested at many levels of patience as they accompany their children through the athletic experience. They need to keep in mind the varying developmental levels of children and respect the variance among all children. Above all, they can be patient and happy with their child's progress as he or she develops on individual timetables. Parents can remind children that improvement comes with practice over time. Parents know their children best and should acknowledge and respect any limitations that emerge. The young gymnast depends on the parent for guidance and support during this demanding activity. Excellence in gymnastics, an art as well as a sport, is elusive. The perfection all competitive gymnasts seek is extremely rare. Young gymnasts will benefit greatly in this quest when parents provide motivational guidance and support. Children should be assured that their self-worth is not based on the height of the jump or the spin of the somersault but rather the effort and attitude in pursuit of improvement.

Additional Coaching and Learning Resources

Many gymnastics clubs have their own websites with photos, information on their activities, and links to other national and international organizations. As of this writing, no one has widely developed a web-based video-clip library of gymnastics routines or skills so that proper execution can be repeatedly observed and analyzed. Instructional video clips on a web page at the club or national level for gymnastics skills instruction could provide a host of learning opportunities for both students and coaches. This resource would also let parents know what types of skills their young gymnasts are working on.

At the United States Military Academy, we have developed a video-based web-page model that we use in many of our skills courses, including a required gymnastics course for freshmen. The website is menu driven with choices by event and routine level. Events are listed along the left side of the screen, and routine numbers are listed across the top. A student first selects the apparatus or event area, then the number corresponding to the routine for that area. A video of the routine then appears within the menu window. Governing gymnastics organizations could model a website based on this format. This would be tremendously beneficial to gymnasts, coaches, and officials. Most of the organizational work has already been done. For example, required skills are already described and categorized in text format on the USA Gymnastics (USAG) national organization's website. The final phase, videotaping the element or skill combination as described in the text and setting up a hyperlink within the web page to the corresponding video clip, is the logical next step. Proper coaching and supervision is still critical. Nevertheless, the integration of Internet technology with a well-supervised program has great potential.

Gymnastics Organizations

Various gymnastics organizations offer services such as continuing education for instructors, safety and training clinics for coaches, and standardized guidelines. Team members often compete under the rules and regulations of different organizations. The following organizations are recognized at both the national and international levels.

USA Gymnastics (USAG)
USAG is the national governing body for gymnastics in the United States.

> USAG National Office:
>
> USA Gymnastics
>
> Pan American Plaza, Suite 300
>
> 201 S. Capitol Avenue
>
> Indianapolis, IN 46225
>
> Phone: 317-237-5050
>
> Fax: 317-237-5069
>
> Website (USA Gymnastics Online): www.usa-gymnastics.org

Amateur Athletic Union (AAU)
AAU Gymnastics provides competition that is divided by athletes' ages and skill levels.

> AAU National Headquarters:
>
> Amateur Athletic Union
>
> c/o Walt Disney World Resort
>
> P.O. Box 10,000
>
> Lake Buena Vista, FL 32830-1000

Phone: 407-934-7200

Fax: 407-934-7242

Website: www.aausports.org

U.S. Association of Independent Gymnastics Clubs (USAIGC)
The USAIGC represents the individual gymnastics clubs in the United States, which are also USAG members.

USAIGC National Headquarters:

235 Pinehurst Road

Wilmington, DE 19803

Toll free: 800-480-0201

Phone: 302-656-3706

Fax: 302-656-8929

Website: www.usaigc.com

Federation Internationale De Gymnastique (FIG)
FIG is the governing body for international gymnastics competition.

Rue des Oeuches 10

Case postale 359

2740 MOUTIER 1 / Switzerland NASTIQUE

Phone: +41 32 494 64 10

Fax: +41 32 494 64 19

Website: www.fig-gymnastics.com

References

Biggs, T., and B. Judge. 1998. Areas of dance as they relate to gymnastics. *Technique* 18 (3): 6-9.

Caine, D., and K. Lindner. 1985. Overuse injuries of growing bones: Is the young female gymnast at risk? *The Physician and Sportsmedicine* 13 (12): 51-54, 56-61, 64.

Fait, H. 1964. *Physical education for the elementary school child*. Philadelphia, PA: W.B. Saunders.

Gallahue, D.L., and J.C. Ozmun. 1998. *Understanding motor development: Infants, children, adolescents, adults*. 4th ed. Boston: WCB/McGraw-Hill.

Martens, R. 1997. *Successful coaching*. 2d ed. Champaign, IL: Human Kinetics.

DANCE

Gayle Kassing

Dance is a natural outlet to express oneself, enhance creativity, gain movement skills, and improve self-confidence. Enjoyed and pursued as a lifelong activity beginning in early childhood and extending through older adult years, dance can be experienced as a leisure-time activity, a component of arts education, a continuing study of dance or dance education, or a personal commitment as an artist. Much of dance instruction and preprofessional training exists in non-school-based programs. These non-school-based dance programs are typically offered in

- private dance studios,
- professional and nonprofessional schools attached to dance companies,
- community arts and recreation organizations, and
- onsite programs in day-care centers.

Each of these non-school-based programs offers dance instruction for different purposes, including dance as recreation and enjoyment, dance as education, or dance as a performing art. Dance technique taught in non-school-based programs may provide

- basic instruction as an introduction to the dance form,
- competency in one or more dance forms to attain entrance into a university dance program, or
- achievement of a high level of professional training in preparation for a dance performance career.

Both non-school-based and school-based dance education programs focus on learning and acquiring skill in performing a variety of dance forms. However, beyond the study of dance technique, students in public school dance programs engage in composing dances, studying about dance and dancers, and learning to appreciate dance performances from a variety of dance forms and cultures. These activities also may be included in non-school-based programs to further enrich students' knowledge of dance (Kassing and Jay, in press).

Private Dance Studios

Dance programs in the private dance studio setting range from recreation and personal enjoyment classes to dance education and preprofessional dance training. When selecting a dance studio for a child, parents should find out the focus of the dance studio. If the focus is on dance as recreation and enjoyment, the instruction is geared to providing basic dance instruction experiences in which the child goes through the process of learning steps, practicing them, and performing them in a dance that is presented for the public.

If the program focuses on dance education, the instruction is geared to the child learning both knowledge about the dance form and how to perform the dance form. In some dance studios, dance education includes learning dance terminology, completing worksheets, and taking tests on terminology. Students may also learn dances from a historical period or an artist's repertoire and gain an understanding about famous dancers, ballets, or contemporary works and artists.

If the dance studio prepares students for the dance profession, the technical demands of the dance form must meet the requirements for entry level into the profession or for acceptance into a college program. The purpose of the dance curriculum in this type of program is to develop the advanced dancer. The focus is on gaining technique, learning choreography, and performing throughout the year. The commitment to rehearsals and performances is significant and the training rigorous when attempting to attain this high level of technical proficiency and artistic development. Often, preprofessional training centers are associated with professional dance organizations.

Studio and Public Performances, Recitals and Competitions in Private Dance Studios

At the end of the year, there is generally a public performance or recital. Usually, the teacher teaches dance technique throughout the year and several months before the recital, the students learn the dance they will perform. The recital is the culminating event of the year; presented on stage, in costume with lighting and often sets for the public. In other non-school-based settings, performances are either on stage for the public or in the classroom. The formality of the performance with costumes, lighting and sets depends upon the organization and the teacher.

During the year, some programs offer parent observation classes. At these times, parents are invited to observe the class. This is an opportunity to see your child's progress and interaction in the classroom.

Unique to the dance studio is dance competitions. For some dance studios this is an important performance outlet. Dance competitions have proliferated and can be found at the regional, state and national levels. Different organizations provide dance competitions such as companies dedicated to producing these events, nationally known dance teachers and professional dance studio organizations.

Dance studios may select students for competition training. Participating in dance competition groups requires enrolling in certain technique classes, additional classes to learn the dances that will be performed and committing a great deal of extra time to rehearsals and to the competition. Students learn the performance process and how to work with others in dance ensemble. Obviously they increase their technical and performance skills and learn showmanship. Some dance studios are committed to competitions while others include it as an option for their students.

Professional and Nonprofessional Schools Affiliated With Dance Companies

Many professional and nonprofessional dance companies have a dance school connected to the company. These schools serve several functions, including

- providing dance instruction and dance education to the community;
- giving teaching jobs to company members; and
- supporting the dance company's productions with additional dancers from the school, revenues, and in the form of additional audience members.

The dance instruction in these schools is geared to dance as a performing art. The teachers are professional dancers from the company or dance teachers affiliated with the company or its artistic direction. These types of schools focus on technique and performance to provide preprofessional training for individuals aspiring to a career in dance.

Most nonprofessional dance companies are civic ballets. These companies are usually an outgrowth of a dance studio or a separate not-for-profit community-based civic ballet or nonprofessional dance company that draws from the dance studios in the area to provide a performance outlet for dancers. Nonprofessional dance companies are often funded through arts council grants at the local and state level. They depend on parent supporters and volunteers to mount productions for the community. The dancers gain invaluable experience by participating in dance performances in a variety of settings and bring dance performance to various segments of the community. Furthermore, these companies provide performance experiences that prepare dancers for college and professional dance companies. The teachers in these settings are either professional dancers who perform in a dance company or dance teachers who have extensive knowledge of dance technique required for professional-caliber performances.

Community Recreation and Arts Programs

Community-based dance programs, such as those conducted in community arts and recreation programs and offered by the YMCA and park districts, generally focus on basic instruction in dance as recreation, enjoyment, or self-development. In settings such as the YMCA, parks and recreation centers, and other community programs, dance programs are generally introductory in nature. These programs usually have short classes and last for only a few weeks. They may or may not offer sessions that provide instruction beyond the beginning level. Typically, these sessions provide a way for children to learn the basics and see if they wish to continue participation. The offerings of these recreation programs depend on the availability of instructors and the programming commitments of the organization. Performance and performing opportunities may or may not be an important aspect of these programs. Teachers in these programs are from the community or dance studios and vary in background and level of training.

Community arts programs focus on dance either as an art form or for basic instruction. Dance in community arts programs may be offered as a separate program or as part of another department such as drama or music. In the latter case, dance is often integrated into other arts productions such as musical theater programs and productions. Teachers in these settings may be trained in dance or in several art forms, or they may come from the private studio sector.

Programs in Day-Care and Preschool Centers

Dance is offered to preschoolers in some day-care centers and preschool settings. These programs usually consist of basic movement exploration activities. Teachers in these settings may be early childhood instructors, dance specialists, or dance teachers from a local dance studio.

Many types of dance instruction for children are appropriate, but the teacher and parents must be aware of the type of program being offered and evaluate whether this type of program meets the abilities, needs, and interests of each child. In addition, the teacher should be qualified to provide high-quality instruction and understand movement and dance as they relate to the developmental level and age of the children being taught.

Common Types of Dance Instruction for Children and Youth

Dance instruction for children and youth varies considerably. This section describes the dance forms most often taught in non-school-based dance programs for preschool children through teenagers. Except for pointe work, which has traditionally been performed by females, all of these dance forms are appropriate for both boys and girls.

Preschool Children

Dance instruction usually begins at age 3. Some programs are specifically dedicated to the 2- to 2½-year-old. These classes are very short and may be shared experiences with a parent, such as a "mommy and me" class that focuses on basic movement exploration and games.

Offerings or titles for dance forms at this age are based on the teacher's background or on what is popular in the region or community. Creative movement, pre-ballet, and kinderdance are common types of dance programs for the preschool and lower-elementary school child. Course content depends on the teacher's background. These courses often include movement exploration, learning basic dance movements from ballet and other dance forms, or a combination of both.

Tap dance is a popular dance form for preschoolers to increase rhythm and coordination. For preschoolers, tap dance is often taught in combination with songs or presented as "creative tap," in which the teacher creates a story to which the dancers tap out the sounds.

Combination classes are popular offerings in the dance studio. These classes offer instruction in two different dance forms or in one dance form and one other movement experience (often, tumbling or acrobatics). Because the young child's attention span is less than 20 minutes, many combination classes are 45 minutes to one hour long, with a rest period between the two dance forms to change shoes.

Elementary School–Age Children

Creative dance serves as a natural continuation of creative movement for the lower-elementary school child. In creative dance, the child learns basic movement and dance steps and explores how to create dances and how to collaborate in groups to create dances. This type of program is more prevalent in school dance programs than in non-school-based dance programs.

In most non-school-based programs, the emphasis is on pre-ballet and tap and may include tumbling or acrobatics. Creative dance may be offered, depending on the program. Combination classes continue for lower-elementary school children in the same forms as for preschoolers.

Upper-Elementary, Middle, and High School Students

Older children can choose from a variety of dance forms, such as modern dance, jazz dance, tap dance, ballet and pointe, and partnering.

Modern Dance

Modern dance is the natural outgrowth of creative movement and dance. This dance form is appropriate for upper-elementary through high school students. The types of modern dance taught in non-school-based programs depend on the teacher and his or her background. Many non-school-based programs include the study of modern dance to broaden the students' knowledge of dance and to provide another option to the traditional study of ballet, tap, and jazz in the dance studio. Modern dance techniques stem from the dance artist or choreographer who developed them. For example, Martha Graham created the Graham technique; José Limón developed the Limón Technique. Generally, dance teachers are trained in one or more modern dance techniques. They either teach one specific style or select from a variety of techniques and styles, blending them together or interpreting them from their own points of view.

Jazz Dance

Jazz dance is a popular dance form for students from upper-elementary school through high school and seems to gain popularity in the upper grades. Jazz dance includes a range of styles from which the teacher selects as appropriate for the age and technical level of the child. Jazz dance is the basis for musical theatre dance, dance lines, dance teams in high school, swing choirs, and other concert and entertainment dance forms. As with modern dance, jazz dance techniques are an outgrowth of jazz dance artists and choreographers. Jazz dance has an extensive range, from the techniques of traditional masters such as Luigi and Mattox to the latest styles seen on television and in the movies. The jazz dance styles that dance teachers use in their teaching and choreography are continually changing, most often reflecting personal style, which often blends ballet, modern dance, and an amalgamation of influences from social dance and different popular entertainment mediums.

Tap Dance

Tap dance instruction spans from prekindergarten through college-age students. It is popular with a wide range of ages, from preschool children to adults. Tap dance provides a strong basis for work in musicals and entertainment settings; training in tap dance is necessary if the student wishes to pursue a career in either of these fields.

Ballet

Ballet is appropriate for children 8 years old or older. Ballet for the lower-elementary school years is pre-ballet training in preparation for the study of classical ballet. If the focus is ballet as dance education or career training, the number and intensity of the sessions should be considered. During the first year, one class a week for an hour would be appropriate. Then classes may be increased to two classes per week for an hour and 15 minutes followed by three classes per week that last an hour and a half. More classes per week can be added to increase the training effect; however, the intensity of the classes in relation to the growing child should be considered. As children grow and develop, physical activity such as ballet can contribute to strong bones and muscle strength. However, too intensive dance training may contribute to lapses in other areas. Parents should weigh the number of dance classes and their intensity against the amount of time children spend in other activities, play, school, and sleep. A balance of activities combined with proper nutrition to sustain all these activities will support proper growth and the physical and emotional health of the child.

Ballet training can be based on the background of the teacher or the philosophy of the studio, or it can be based on a standard training syllabus such as those from the Royal Academy of Dancing or the Cecchetti Council of America. The Royal Academy of Dancing and the Cecchetti Council of America provide equally fine training methods, though they differ in their approach and syllabi. Using a syllabus, students complete levels of study and are tested on standards provided by the syllabus before moving to the next level of difficulty. If the teacher uses an acknowledged syllabus, he or she has passed teacher certification examinations to teach the syllabus. If the teacher does not use a syllabus, he or she may have studied with professionals and may be continuing studies at professional dance organizations or with a university program.

If the student wants to become a professional dancer, the teacher is key. The teacher must have the knowledge and experience to guide the student from a beginning to a professional level. The teacher must have the capabilities, strengths, and abilities to provide sound instruction based on a thorough understanding of dance science, applied kinesiology, and development of artistry.

Pointe Technique

Pointe technique should be a natural outgrowth of ballet studies. The age to begin training in pointe varies with each child and will depend on the child's physical development, technical strength, and ability. Children typically are not ready to begin pointe technique until $10\,^1/_2$ - 12 years of age.

Learning to dance en pointe requires a knowledgeable instructor who understands how to properly train students in this technique. Deciding whether a child should participate in pointe technique should not be done lightly, as serious risks may be involved if the student undertakes this technique too young and without enough ballet training. Likewise, the child should not be pushed too fast in pointe technique for the same reasons. The child should be able to perform ballet movements competently in ballet slippers before attempting them en pointe. Overweight children should not dance en pointe because this can place them in danger of injury. Selecting the appropriate shoe for student practice and performance is crucial to good training. Parents and children should consult with a knowledgeable person trained in the proper fitting of pointe shoes. High-quality instruction is essential to developing proper technique and a strong body through these formative years.

Partnering

Partnering, or supported adagio, may be another offering at the dance studio. Learning how to dance in a male and female partnership provides excellent training that can be transferred into other dance forms. The female student should be able to confidently perform en pointe at least at a high intermediate to advanced level. The male dancer should be competent at least at the intermediate level. In beginning partnering, the couple learns supported balances with leg extensions or various poses using different handholds. The next stage is a series of graduated lifts, pirouettes, and carrying movements. The male partner must do weight training to gain the upper-body strength needed to lift the female.

Other Dance Choices

Other dance forms frequently offered in the dance studio include ethnic and recreational dance in a variety of forms such as folk dancing, belly dancing, hula, hip-hop, ballroom, aerobic dance, line dance, dance fitness, and other movement forms such as yoga, stretching, and Pilates. In addition, the dance studio may offer training in cheerleading, pompon squads, dance line, baton twirling, and other dance and movement specialties of the dance teacher.

Age-Appropriate Dance Progression in the Private Studio Setting

In the dance studio setting, age and developmentally appropriate dance classes range from preschool through adults. The dance forms most often found in this setting are traditional dance forms such as ballet, tap, and jazz dance. Creative movement and dance and modern dance are increasingly becoming offerings in the private studio. Other dance forms are offered based upon a teacher's background or interest in the community. In this section, the age of the child is related to participation in appropriate dance forms.

Preschool Classes

2- to 4-Year-Olds

Discussion

Dance programs generally accept children who are 3 to 4 years old. Preschool children most commonly learn creative movement, pre-ballet, tumbling or acrobatics, or tap dance. The classes are held once a week and are often offered together as combination classes to create a 45-minute to one-hour class.

Benefits and Risks

Benefits of dance for young children are many. Young children can learn to enjoy moving and dancing and gain movement confidence. The focus should be on gaining balance, improving coordination, and experiencing movement, not on acquiring dance technique. Children's dance should let children participate as individuals, with little or no attention to ensemble and on-cue performance as part of a group.

Elementary Classes

5- to 7-Year-Olds

Discussion

The types of combination classes offered to 5- to 7-year-olds are similar to those offered to preschoolers. Classes for this age group are often longer than are those for preschoolers, and sometimes the emphasis changes to ballet and tap, away from creative movement and dance.

Benefits and Risks

Ballet classes for this age group should focus on basic movements without stressing turnout or technical aspects. The child's body is not mature enough to meet the demands of this dance form.

Upper-Elementary Classes

8- to 12-Year-Olds

Discussion

By ages 8 to 12, combination classes separate into ballet, tap, jazz, modern dance, acrobatics, and other specialty classes. The classes increase in length from 45 minutes to one hour and often increase in frequency to two times a week. In ballet, the classes extend in length from one hour to an hour and 15 minutes to an hour and a half as the child progresses. After several years of ballet training, depending on the number of classes per week and the physical maturity of the child, pointe technique may be added. The pointe class is often attached to the end of the ballet class, extending the class to 2 hours. Sometimes pointe is offered as a separate class. For the serious dance student, this is an important time to gain appropriate technique and begin developing performance skills.

Deciding when to begin pointe technique is the major safety consideration for this age group. The physical maturity of the child and the amount of previous study will determine when a child can begin pointe work. Pointe technique should be attempted only after the child demonstrates consistent and competent ballet technique so that the transition is gradual, as discussed previously.

Benefits and Risks

Between the ages of 8 and 12, children experience growth spurts. Parents should tell the teacher when their children are experiencing growth spurts. To prevent injury, the amount, types, and intensity of stretching, high leg extensions, and splits should be monitored during these periods. The number of ballet classes per week should increase gradually and should be balanced with other dance forms and adequate time for the child to rest between strenuous classes and rehearsals. Students should warm up before dancing to avoid injury. Although strength, endurance, and technical proficiency are pursued to develop the dancer during these formative years, overuse should be monitored.

For this age group, the dance class and its environment provides a social outlet for developing social and emotional skills. Often the dance studio becomes the place to "hang out" and become part of an extended family environment. Working in performance groups develops teamwork and camaraderie. Children in this age group often have school friends and dance friends.

Pre-Adolescent and Adolescent Classes

12- to 16-Year-Olds

Discussion

Interest in dance training as a recreational activity may wane for 12- to 16-year-olds. But for the serious student, this is a time to gain momentum in acquiring a high level of skill and developing artistry. Ballet and pointe technique, jazz dance, modern dance, and tap dance continue to be the most popular dance forms at this age. Some students begin their dance experiences during this age in jazz dance or modern dance because of an interest or as outside training for school-based programs. More experienced students who are committed to becoming professional dancers may prepare for and participate in summer intensive programs that may lead to apprenticeships and later to company positions.

Benefits and Risks

For 12- to 16-year-olds, life is rapidly changing, as are their school and social lives. For some, dance is relinquished so that they can participate in other school activities. For others, dance becomes an even more integral part of their lives as they hone their skills toward a career or for college. Students in this age group must balance their work in the dance studio with their schoolwork and lifestyle.

Students' continued physical development must be considered, as posture, balance, and stretching abilities change with body changes and body image. Teenagers are sometimes mentally and emotionally fragile. Dance can help support a positive self-image and self-confidence through this time of growth and change.

High School to Adult Classes

16- to 18-Year-Olds

Discussion

For students who have studied dance for a number of years, the late high school years are the polishing years. Most often these students are planning to major in dance in college or may enter the profession. Ballet and pointe technique, jazz dance, modern dance, and tap dance continue to be the central dance forms, with specialty classes in hip-hop, ethnic dance, and other dance forms. Students continue to advance their technical studies while working to sharpen their performance artistry to prepare them for their college or professional dance career. Because of the demands of high school and the desire to participate in outside activities, students in this age group who are still dancing are generally committed to dance as a profession. Often, students who attend performing arts high schools continue their studies in their home dance studios to increase the number of classes taken each week.

Intensive summer study at home, at professional programs attached to companies, or with nationally recognized programs can provide additional training to prepare the student for college or entry into the profession.

Benefits and Risks

For these young dancers, the risks continue to include overuse, intensity, and body image. These students' bodies continue to develop, and some dancers experience trauma in coping with their physical maturation. Students may need to come to terms with their body shape, size, and physical attributes to help determine a career focus in or out of dance.

Steps to Finding the Right Dance Studio

When selecting a dance program in a non-school setting, parents should become aware of the type of dance program being offered and if the program and dance instruction is appropriate for the child. Parents can begin the search for dance instruction by reading the yellow page advertisements. Some dance studios simply list their name, while others use display advertisements to indicate the dance forms offered, if the studio or program has performances or participates in competitions, and the credentials of the dance studio teacher. Parents may also find a dance studio based on information from other parents whose children attend dance classes in the area.

Parents can then telephone several dance studio owners or instructors to gain information about the studio, its focus, the types of classes offered to certain age groups, how important competition and the recital experiences are, and other important information such as location, times, and lengths of classes.

Visiting the Dance Program

Parents should visit the dance studio to gain a sense of the atmosphere in the studio. Parents should try to meet the instructor and observe the instructor teach a class of children in the same age group as their child, if possible. Parents may also evaluate whether the studio provides adequate space to move, is clean, provides a variety of activities during the class, has a good teacher-to-student ratio, and ensures that children are actively engaged in moving, rather than standing for long periods waiting their turn, during class time. This visit will give parents a sense of the studio's atmosphere, the teacher, and the instruction given.

Studio brochures or other printed material can also help in determining if the studio is the right place for the child. Most studios or programs produce brochures of their offerings and policies. Parents should try to schedule a short conference with the teacher to learn about recital and other policies. Learning this and other information will help parents make informed decisions as to their children's participation.

Performance Insights

Parents may also evaluate a studio by attending performances of the dance studio or program to see other children of their child's age group perform. Being in a recital can be a positive experience if the child is ready and if the performance experience is handled by the teacher and the studio in a manner that is appropriate for the dancers in that age group. How well the studio or program organizes the dance recital or performance production aspects can be an indication of the professionalism of the organization.

Some studios set a higher priority on producing dance works for dance competition, performances, and the recital than on good dance instruction and developing dance technique to support study beyond the beginning level. If this is the case, parents need to consider if this is the right atmosphere for their children. For children seeking dance training as a recreational outlet, the performance and competition process may be appropriate. If dance is a serious endeavor that the child loves and wants to study, then dance instruction and technique development should have the highest priority and can be balanced with performance and other activities outside the dance class.

Parents should determine the teacher's and studio's position on the importance of performance, competition, and recitals. Parents can then evaluate how these events interface with their own values, beliefs, and lifestyle. Parents may wish to observe such events before making a judgment.

Dance Teacher's Training and Philosophy of Teaching

The dance teacher's background, training, expertise, and interest will determine the curriculum and the focus of the program. Parents should learn what the teacher's credentials are and decide if the credentials support the purpose of the studio.

Dance studio teachers in the private sector are often members of professional dance organizations. These organizations provide continuing education for the dance teacher throughout the year and at annual conventions. Some dance studio teachers have completed university undergraduate or graduate degrees in dance or dance and education. Others, after having performed professionally, have decided to open a dance studio. In community settings, the dance instructor may be a high school dancer, a college student, a dancer, or a person with previous dance or dance performance in their background.

Even in the non-school-based setting, the dance teacher should have had training in dance. More important, the dance teacher should have knowledge of dance science, including kinesiology, injury prevention, and a thorough understanding of how to teach different dance forms to different age groups. Knowledge of a child's growth and development is crucial to good dance instruction. Parents should remember that they are paying for an expert to teach their child. Dance and the teacher's instruction mold the young person's body physically. Dance teachers must be able to explain how to do exercises properly to avoid stress and injury and to create a strong technique. Parents can find out what constitutes proper and correct training by reading some of the references provided at the end of this chapter. These books outline what the teacher should do in the class.

When to Enroll in a Dance Program

The best time of year to enroll your child in a dance studio or other non-school-based dance program is the fall, since this is when most programs start for the year. Non-school dance programs have sessions of varying lengths that range from 5 to 7 weeks, half-year terms, or full year programs. The longer sessions generally culminate in a performance or recital. Many non-school-based dance programs offer summer sessions, intensive workshops, or dance camps. These summer programs can also serve as continued training for dance competitions and performance groups during the regular school year.

Additional Resources

Because the dance studio is a service business, the Better Business Bureau or chamber of commerce can provide business information. The artistic community can provide information regarding the artistic and technical quality of the dance program. The teacher should have credentials from a university or show continued study; however, parents remain the judge of the teaching styles used with students in the classroom and the learning atmosphere created in the dance class, the studio, or program.

Magazines such as *Dance Teacher* can provide more information about the profession of dance teaching in the dance studio.

Reference

Kassing G., and D. Jay. In press. *Dance teaching methods and curriculum design*. Champaign, IL: Human Kinetics.

Other Books

Hatchett, F., and N.M. Gitlin. 2000. *Frank Hatchett's jazz dance*. Champaign, IL: Human Kinetics.

Kassing, G., and D. Jay. 1998. *Teaching beginning ballet technique*. Champaign, IL: Human Kinetics.

Minton, S. 1996. *Modern dance*. Champaign, IL: Human Kinetics.

Purcell, T. 1994. *Teaching children dance: Becoming a master teacher*. Champaign, IL: Human Kinetics.

Appendix

Progression of Physical Activity Skills for Team Sports, Gymnastics, and Dance

Training Activities	18 mos-3 yrs	4-5 yrs	6-7 yrs	8-12 yrs	13-16 yrs	17-18 yrs
Kinesthetic awareness exercises (rolling, twisting, and turning)	T, G, D	T, G, D	T, G, D	T, G, D	T, G, D	T, G, D
Basic gymnastics skills (body position, tightness, and control)	T, G, D	T, G, D	T, G, D	T, G, D	T, G, D	T, G, D
Flexibility training	T, G, D	T, G, D	T, G, D	T, G, D	T, G, D	T, G, D
General fitness skills (running and jumping)		T, G, D	T, G, D	T, G, D	T, G, D	T, G, D
Ballet and dance lessons			T, G, D	T, G, D	T, G, D	G, D
Agility drills			T, G, D	T, G, D	T, G, D	T, G, D
Tumbling			T, G, D	T, G, D	T, G, D	T, G, D
Trampoline activities			T, G, D	T, G, D	T, G, D	T, G, D
General strength skills (pull-ups, sit-ups, and push-ups)				T, G, D	T, G, D	T, G, D
Skill-specific body, trunk and leg circuit training				T, G, D	T, G, D	T, G, D

T = Team sports
G = Gymnastics
D = Dance

Contributors

Danny R. Mielke has over 30 years of experience as a professor and a teacher of physical education and holds a doctoral degree with expertise in the area of movement development. He continues his passion for physical education as a professor of physical education and health at Eastern Oregon University.

Susan M. Tendy is the Director of Assessment for the Department of Physical Education, United States Military Academy at Westpoint. She has taught gymnastics at the higher education level since 1970 and is a well-respected leader and advocate for gymnastics. In 2002, in recognition of her teaching excellence in physical education and gymnastics, Tendy received the U.S. Military Academy's Anderson Achievement Award for Excellence in Teaching.

Carmine Giglio is the Assistant Men's Gymnastics Coach and physical educator for the United States Military Academy at Westpoint. He has been involved in the sport of gymnastics for 23 years, first as a competitive gymnast, and later working in a private setting as owner and coach of his own gymnastics club.

Gayle Kassing has taught dance technique and pedagogy, dance methods, and curriculum design in dance teacher education preparation programs in both physical education and fine arts departments for more than 25 years. She is currently putting her experience and knowledge in dance and physical education to work as an acquisitions editor in Human Kinetics' division of Health, Physical Education, Recreation and Dance. She is also completing her second book with Human Kinetics entitled *Dance Teaching Methods and Curriculum Design*.

About the Editor

Patricia A. Sullivan, EdD, is the associate director of health, physical education, recreation and dance at the ERIC Clearinghouse on Teaching and Teacher Education. She has over 30 years of experience in teaching; coaching; and working with teachers, coaches, and parents. She is a professor of exercise science at George Washington University. Dr. Sullivan is a member of the American Alliance for Health, Physical Education, Recreation and Dance; the National Association for Girls and Women in Sport; and the National Association for Sport and Physical Education. She recently completed a term as president of the National Council for the Accreditation of Coaching Education.

*You'll find
other outstanding
physical education resources at*

www.HumanKinetics.com

In the U.S. call

800-747-4457

Australia 08 8277 1555
Canada 800-465-7301
Europe .... +44 (0) 113 255 5665
New Zealand 09-523-3462

HUMAN KINETICS
The Information Leader in Physical Activity
P.O. Box 5076 • Champaign, IL 61825-5076 USA